The American Colonies

The Massachusetts Bay Colony

by Kathleen W. Deady

Consultant:
William M. Fowler Jr.
Director
Massachusetts Historical Society
Boston, Massachusetts

Capstone
press

Mankato, Minnesota

Fact Finders is published by Capstone Press,
151 Good Counsel Drive, P.O. Box 669, Mankato, Minnesota 56002.
www.capstonepress.com

Library of Congress Cataloging-in-Publication Data
Deady, Kathleen W.
    The Massachusetts Bay colony / by Kathleen W. Deady.
    p. cm. — (Fact Finders. American colonies)
    Includes bibliographical references and index.
    ISBN 0-7368-2676-9
    1. Massachusetts—History—Colonial period, ca. 1600-1775—Juvenile literature. I.
    Title.II. Series: American colonies (Capstone Press)
F67.D285 2006
974.4'02—dc22   2004028657
Summary: An introduction to the history, government, economy, resources, and people of
    the Massachusetts Bay Colony. Includes maps and charts.

Editorial Credits
Mandy Marx, editor; Jennifer Bergstrom, set designer, illustrator, and book designer;
    Bobbi J. Dey, book designer; Jo Miller, photo researcher/photo editor

Photo Credits
Cover image: Boston Tea Party, American colonists cheer as demonstrators dressed as
    Indians throw tea from British ships, Corbis/Bettmann

Bridgeman Art Library/Private Collection, 26
Corbis/Bettmann, 23, 27; Burstein Collection, 18
The Granger Collection, New York, 11, 14, 15, 22
National Archives and Records Administration, 29 (right)
Neg. no. 1582, courtesy the Library, American Museum of Natural History, 4–5
Northwind Picture Archives, 12–13, 16–17, 21, 29 (left)
Tara Prindle, 6, 7

1 2 3 4 5 6 10 09 08 07 06 05

Table of Contents

Chapter 1

Massachusetts' First People

Massachusetts has been home to American Indians for thousands of years. In southeastern Massachusetts, three large tribes once shared the land. They were the Massachuset, the Nauset, and the Wampanoag. These tribes had similar customs and spoke the same language. The Wampanoag people made up the largest group.

Before Europeans came, more than 12,000 Wampanoag lived in southeastern Massachusetts. Villages were ruled by leaders called sachems. The sachems answered to the Grand Sachem. He was the most powerful Wampanoag leader.

The Wampanoag lived in villages around what is now Massachusetts Bay.

Wampanoag Way of Life

Between 100 and 400 people lived in each Wampanoag village. Their homes were large, wooden domes covered by woven mats or bark. The Wampanoag called them wetus.

In fall and winter, the Wampanoag lived in the forest. Men hunted deer, wolves, bears, and other animals.

The Wampanoag spent most of their time outside. Wetus were used mainly for sleeping. ↓

The Wampanoag moved to the Atlantic coast in the spring. There, men fished and gathered shellfish. Women grew squash, corn, and beans.

European Arrival

In the early 1600s, Europeans explored the Massachusetts area. Without knowing it, the explorers carried European diseases with them.

The Wampanoag could not fight the diseases. By the time English settlers came, the illnesses had killed over half of the Wampanoag.

▲ Wampanoag women made clay pots for storing fruits, vegetables, and herbs.

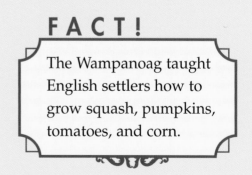

FACT!

The Wampanoag taught English settlers how to grow squash, pumpkins, tomatoes, and corn.

Chapter 2

Early Settlers

In the early 1600s, English law forced people to belong to the Church of England. Some people disagreed with this law. One group left England and moved to Holland. Unhappy there, they decided to go to North America. Today we call these people the Pilgrims.

Reaching America

The Pilgrims had a hard time getting to America. They set sail in September 1620, on the *Speedwell* and the *Mayflower*. They soon found out the *Speedwell* leaked. The Pilgrims left that ship behind and squeezed into the *Mayflower*.

The Proclamation of 1763 set colonial borders. Massachusetts included what later became the state of Maine. ➡

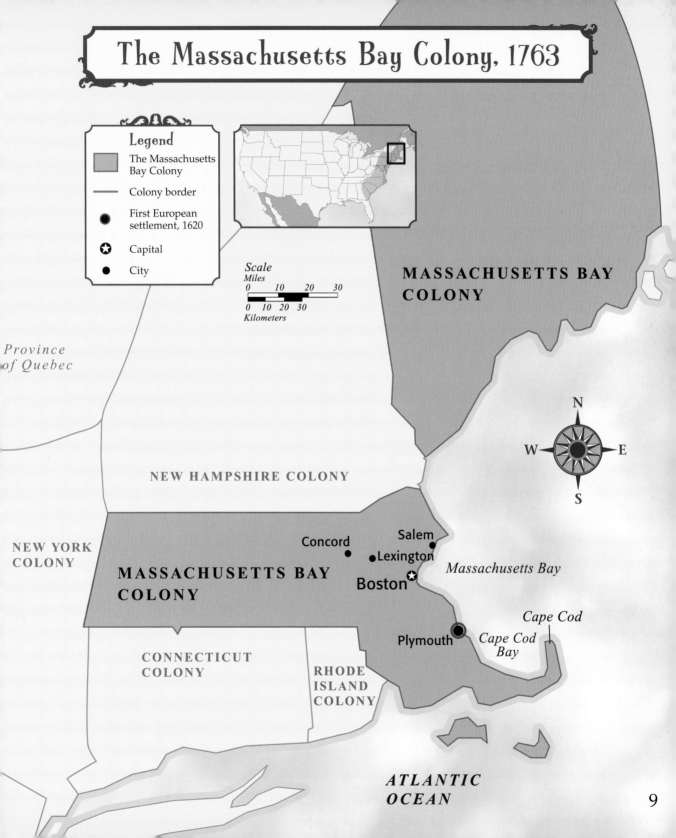

The Massachusetts Bay Colony, 1763

Legend

The Massachusetts Bay Colony

Colony border

● First European settlement, 1620

✪ Capital

● City

Scale
Miles
0 10 20 30

0 10 20 30
Kilometers

Province of Quebec

MASSACHUSETTS BAY COLONY

N
W — E
S

NEW HAMPSHIRE COLONY

NEW YORK COLONY

MASSACHUSETTS BAY COLONY

Concord ●

Salem ●

● Lexington

Massachusetts Bay

✪ **Boston**

CONNECTICUT COLONY

RHODE ISLAND COLONY

Cape Cod

Plymouth ● *Cape Cod Bay*

ATLANTIC OCEAN

The *Mayflower* reached America in November. But wind had blown the ship north of where the Pilgrims wanted to be. Tired and low on supplies, they decided to stay. The Pilgrims called their settlement the Plymouth Colony.

The winter of 1620 was hard. The Pilgrims were not ready for the cold and snow. Half of them died from sickness or lack of food.

Population Growth of the Massachusetts Bay Colony

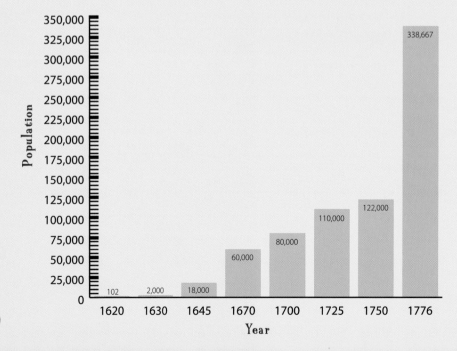

The Pilgrims' Hero

In March, an American Indian named Squanto came to Plymouth. He had visited England and learned to speak English. Squanto taught the Pilgrims where to hunt and how to grow new crops. By fall, the Pilgrims had enough food to last the winter. They held a feast of thanksgiving.

Puritan Arrival

In 1630, **Puritans** settled near Plymouth. They were part of the Massachusetts Bay Company. Soon, Puritans outnumbered Pilgrims. In 1691, the Massachusetts Bay Colony took over Plymouth.

Squanto showed the Pilgrims how to plant new crops and use fish as fertilizer. ➤

Chapter 3

Colonial Life

Most Massachusetts colonists spent their days working on the farm. But Sundays were spent in town. Colonists went to the meetinghouse for church. Services lasted most of the day. After church, colonists met on a central grassy area that served as a park. It was called the town common.

Life in Massachusetts

Early Massachusetts homes had one room. They had large fireplaces and low ceilings to keep in heat. Colonists used the fireplace for cooking and for warmth in winter. Because glass was expensive, windows were covered by cloth or wood.

Boston was one of the few large cities in the Massachusetts Bay Colony.

Colonists' days were filled with hard work. Men cleared forests for farming and built homes. Women spun plants called flax into linen to make clothes. They also cooked, cleaned, and cared for children.

Children helped parents whenever they could. Girls learned to cook, clean, and sew at an early age. Boys helped their fathers farm and care for animals.

Education

Puritans believed faith came from reading the Bible. Because of this belief, they taught children to read.

In 1647, the government passed the School Law. It required towns with more than 50 families to build schools. The schools were paid for with **taxes**. This was the first public school system in America.

Boys and girls were taught differently. Girls learned reading, sewing, and some math. Boys were taught reading, languages, science, math, and history. This knowledge prepared some boys for college.

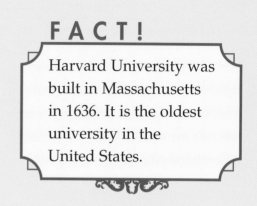

In the Massachusetts Bay Colony, boys and girls went to school together. But they learned different subjects. ▼

Chapter 4

Work and Trade

Many of Massachusetts' first settlers were farmers. They grew fruits and vegetables and raised cattle to feed their families.

Massachusetts was one of the New England Colonies. Farming was difficult in that area. The growing season was short, and the soil was rocky. By the mid-1600s, people began looking for work other than farming.

Codfish filled the waters off the coast of Massachusetts. Fishers caught and dried codfish. They sold it to traders. Traders sold the fish to people in England. As this trade grew, many fishers and traders became wealthy.

Farmers in Massachusetts had to dig large stones out of the land before they could plant crops.

In the 1640s, Massachusetts colonists began mining bog iron. This heavy metal was found in and around the Saugus and Taunton rivers. Colonists used the metal to make anchors, nails, and tools.

As early as 1650, Boston Harbor was crowded with ships.

Business Booms

In the mid-1600s, a pattern of trade began in the colonies. Colonists got molasses from Caribbean islands called the West Indies. They made molasses into rum. Rum was traded for slaves from Africa. Some slaves were sold in the Southern Colonies to work on large farms. Colonists traded the other slaves for more molasses from the West Indies.

In the early 1700s, Boston, Massachusetts, was New England's business center. There were many merchants and traders. Shipbuilding had become a major industry. Boston's nine shipyards built more ships than all the other colonies combined.

Most Massachusetts colonists did not own slaves. There were no large farms for them to work on, like those in Southern Colonies.

Some families did have **indentured servants**. These servants worked unpaid for a fixed number of years to pay off their debts.

Massachusetts Bay Colony's Exports

Agricultural Export
wool

Industrial Exports
ships
iron

Natural Resource Exports
fish
timber products

Chapter 5

Community and Faith

Life in Massachusetts centered around the Puritan faith. All rules and activities were shaped by Puritan beliefs.

Puritan Beliefs and Rules

The Puritans lived by strict rules of the church. Everyone went to church on Sunday. Children who fell asleep in church were hit on the head with a stick. Men could not have long hair or kiss their wives in public. Women were not allowed to wear lace. Often, people were fined or whipped for breaking these rules.

Many Massachusetts colonists came to America to be free to practice their religion.

▲ House raising parties were a combination of work and fun.

Work and Play

In spite of strict rules, Puritans still had fun. Many times they combined work with pleasure.

Parties for building barns and houses were common. At these parties, men worked to raise a building frame. Women spent the day cooking a meal. After the work was done, everyone enjoyed a feast.

Leaving Massachusetts

Some Massachusetts colonists disagreed with the Puritan way of life. The Puritans did not allow people to express different beliefs.

People who disagreed with Puritan ways often left or were thrown out of Massachusetts. Some of them started new settlements in the New Hampshire and Rhode Island colonies.

Rule-breakers were often put in stocks to be mocked by others. ▼

Chapter 6

Becoming a State

Massachusetts colonists governed themselves for 54 years. In 1684, King James II of England took away their power. He made Massachusetts a royal colony. But the colonists had tasted **independence**, and they wanted it back.

Road to Revolution

During the 1700s, Britain fought France for more land in North America. These battles were called the French and Indian wars. In 1763, Britain won.

To pay for the wars, Britain taxed the colonists on paper, sugar, and tea. Since they had no say in British government, many colonists felt the taxes were unfair.

Massachusetts was the first New England colony to form. It was also where the Revolutionary War began. ➤

The Thirteen Colonies, 1763

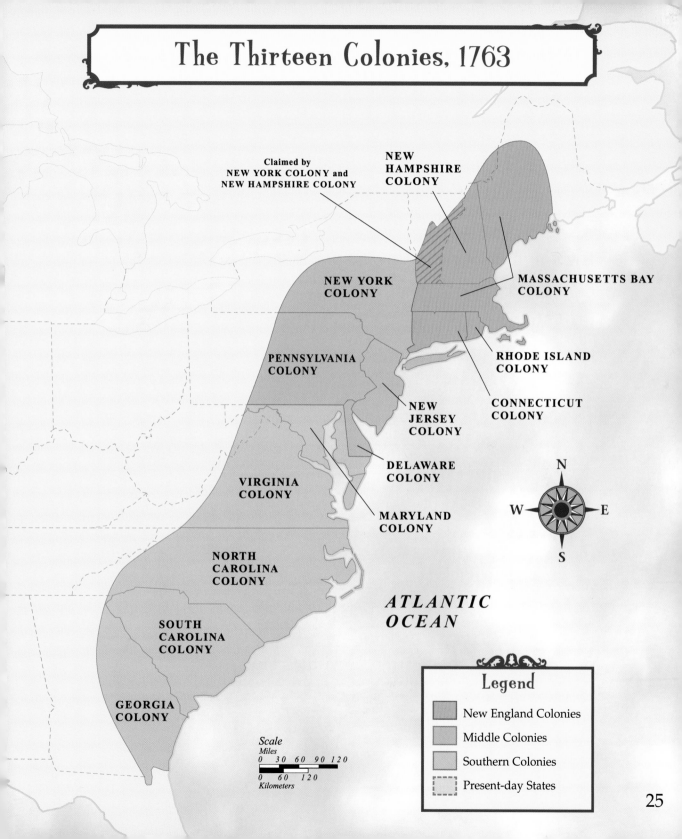

Claimed by
NEW YORK COLONY and
NEW HAMPSHIRE COLONY

NEW HAMPSHIRE COLONY

NEW YORK COLONY

MASSACHUSETTS BAY COLONY

PENNSYLVANIA COLONY

RHODE ISLAND COLONY

CONNECTICUT COLONY

NEW JERSEY COLONY

DELAWARE COLONY

VIRGINIA COLONY

MARYLAND COLONY

NORTH CAROLINA COLONY

SOUTH CAROLINA COLONY

GEORGIA COLONY

ATLANTIC OCEAN

N
W   E
S

Scale
Miles
0 30 60 90 120

0   60   120
Kilometers

Legend

New England Colonies

Middle Colonies

Southern Colonies

Present-day States

25

Massachusetts colonists were angry about the taxes. To protest, they threw a shipload of tea into Boston Harbor. This act became known as the Boston Tea Party.

King George III of England punished the colonists for the Boston Tea party. He closed Boston Harbor. Massachusetts' trade was cut off. People in other colonies tried to help the citizens of Boston. They sent them food and other supplies.

The Boston Tea Party is the most famous protest of the Revolution. ▼

In 1774, the colonies sent **representatives** to the Continental Congress. These men sent a list of demands to the king. But King George III would not give in.

The conflict between the colonies and Britain turned into war in 1775. Congress passed the Declaration of Independence in July 1776.

After years of fighting, America won the war in 1783. The nation's leaders wrote the United States **Constitution** in 1787. It created the U.S. government. Massachusetts approved the Constitution on February 6, 1788. It was the sixth state to join the United States.

▲ The first shots of the Revolutionary War were fired in Lexington, Massachusetts, on April 19, 1775.

FACT!

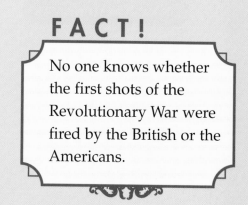

No one knows whether the first shots of the Revolutionary War were fired by the British or the Americans.

Fast Facts

Name
The Massachusetts Bay Colony

Location
New England

Dates of Founding
1620—Plymouth Colony
1630—Massachusetts
       Bay Colony

First Settlements
Pilgrims—Plymouth Colony
Puritans—Boston

Colony's Founders
Pilgrims and Puritans

Religious Faith
Puritan

Agricultural Products
Timber, wool

Major Industries
Fishing, shipbuilding,
ironworks

Population in 1776
338,667 people

Statehood
February 6, 1788
(6th state)

Time Line

1630
Puritans start
the Massachusetts
Bay Colony.

1707
An Act of Union unites
England, Wales, and
Scotland; they become the
Kingdom of Great Britain.

1763
Proclamation of 1763
sets colonial borders
and provides land for
American Indians.

1783
America wins the
Revolutionary War.

1776
Declaration of
Independence is
approved in July.

1620
Pilgrims land in
Massachusetts and
start Plymouth Colony.

1775
First shots of the
Revolutionary War are
fired in Lexington,
Massachusetts.

1788
On February 6,
Massachusetts is
the sixth state
to join the
United States.

1691
Plymouth Colony joins
Massachusetts Bay Colony.

29

Glossary

constitution (kon-stuh-TOO-shuhn)—the system of laws in a state or country that state the rights of the people and the powers of the government

indentured servant (in-DEN-churd SUR-vuhnt)—someone who agrees to work for another person for a certain length of time in exchange for travel expenses, food, or housing

independence (in-di-PEN-duhnss)—being free from the control of other people

Puritan (PYOOR-uh-tuhn)—a group of Protestants who sought simple church services and a strict moral code

representative (rep-ri-ZEN-tuh-tiv)—someone who is chosen to speak or act for others

taxes (TAKS-uhs)—money that people and businesses must pay to support a government

Internet Sites

FactHound offers a safe, fun way to find Internet sites related to this book. All of the sites on FactHound have been researched by our staff.

Here's how:

1. Visit *www.facthound.com*
2. Type in this special code **0736826769** for age-appropriate sites. Or enter a search word related to this book for a more general search.
3. Click on the **Fetch It** button.

FactHound will fetch the best sites for you!

Read More

Lassieur, Allison. *The Voyage of the Mayflower.* Graphic History. Mankato, Minn.: Capstone Press, 2006.

Lilly, Melinda. *Pilgrims in America.* Rourke Discovery Library. Vero Beach, Fla.: Rourke, 2003.

Sateren, Shelley Swanson. *Going to School in Colonial America.* Going to School in History. Mankato, Minn.: Capstone Press, 2002.

Index